THE FORGETFUL ORGANIZATION

How an Organization Struggles to Remember Itself

Stephen Capizzano

A Fairytale For Those Who Still Have A Wish

Leaning Rock Press

Leaning Rock Press, LLC
Box 44
Gales Ferry, CT 06335
www.leaningrockpress.com

978-1-950323-10-4, Hardcover
978-1-950323-11-1, Softcover

Publisher's Cataloging-In-Publication Data
(Prepared by The Donohue Group, Inc.)

Names: Capizzano, Stephen, author.
Title: The forgetful organization : an organization's struggle to remember itself / Stephen Capizzano.
Description: Gales Ferry, CT : Leaning Rock Press, [2020] | "A Fairytale For Those Who Still Have A Wish." | Includes bibliographical references.
Identifiers: ISBN 9781950323104 (hardcover) | ISBN 9781950323111 (softcover)
Subjects: LCSH: Organizational commitment. | Corporate culture. | Employee loyalty. | Leadership.
Classification: LCC HD58.7 .C36 2020 | DDC 658.3--dc23

Library of Congress Control Number: 2020911627

Printed in the United States of America

To My Wife, Suzanne,
Who Has Made Me a Better Man Through Her Fairytale

PREFACE

It is a moment I will always remember. I had been without power for thirteen days in a small cabin in the woods in southern New Hampshire; but the house was built for just such conditions as it had gas lights, two wood stoves and a bathroom that ran on a battery. But it was what happened in one particular moment on that 13th day that I truly remember. With the power still down, I had gone into a room and innocently flicked on the light switch. Thirteen days without power, but I still had that habit. I stood there for a few seconds realizing how absurd my gesture had been.

I am not a writer of fairy tales, although this is one and I am not a philosopher, although I am writing about Aristotle, what I am is a man who has worked all his life and in that working I have observed many of the absurdities that go with working with others. In that moment of flicking on the light switch, my fairy tale became real and I realized something fundamental to my life and work.

We have all been told, over and over again, what it is that can make for a better work place environment, but whether we are in an organization of 10, 100 or a thousand, we find we always come up against the same personalities and the pressures. Part of our dilemma is that we want to make it easy but living a fairy tale is never easy but what is true about each and every fairytale, is that dragons can be beaten.

I recommend reading the first chapter out loud as if you were reading to a child and, in doing so, find your place in your fairytale.

Stephen Capizzano

"Fairytales are more than true:
Not because they tell us that dragons exist,
But because they tell us that dragons can be beaten."

G.K. Chesterton (Neil Gaiman)

Chapter 1

Only in a Fairy Tale

A long time ago, when the world was a much different place, there lived an Organization.

In this organization lived many good people of different shapes, sizes and dispositions, who wanted only the best for themselves and the people they loved. However, as if under a spell, something strange seemed to happen to all of these good people, they fell sound asleep.

Now it certainly did not look as if they were asleep. They continued to move, have conversations, and even get a paycheck at the end of the week, but alas, asleep they were.

This sleep was not a sleep in the usual sense of lying in bed with eyes closed, no, this sleep was the kind one recognizes upon waking from a daydream. And during this sleep, all these good people did their work, had their meetings and took their breaks as if the dream they were in was real.

One day, some of these good people began to recognize they were in a dream-like state and began to get an uneasy feeling, a most uncomfortable feeling, and a sense that this is not the way it is supposed to be. With this uneasiness, something began to stir, and certain individuals, faintly at first began to hear an echo coming from somewhere deep within each one of them. This echo, starting as a simple vibration, began to get louder, forming words, and as the words became clearer their eyes opened with understanding and they began to smile as they realized what was being said:

"Awake, Awake, your prince has arrived."

"Looking like Lethe, see the lake
A conscious slumber seems to take
And would not, for the world, awake."

Edgar Allen Poe

Chapter 2

What We Are

What a strange way to begin a book about organizations but whether one knows it or not, each organization is living out its own fairy tale; a fairy tale that supports a powerful reality unknown to most of us in the sleepiness of our daily work. Our interactions with co-workers and management can become our own individual fairy tale filled with childhood fears and personal demons acted out on the adult stage of life; the only difference from childhood is that the stage is now our place of work. This new-found understanding of sleep is immersed in our need for self-preservation and self-interest and it is only in our awakening from this sleep that an organization can turn toward a grander vision of excellence. I believe a true understanding of organizations begins with one simple sentence:

We are in essence sleeping beauties waiting to be awakened by our prince.

In our hardened business culture, this may be an unusual way to start our story but join me in this exploration and if you are in the right place and your wish is strong, maybe the prince will awaken you.

"We are such stuff that dreams are made on:
and our little life is rounded by a sleep."
Shakespeare

Chapter 3

Stirring

Having had a fondness for fairy tales, one in particular, Sleeping Beauty has always drawn my attention much more than others for two reasons.

The first is that not only does the princess fall asleep but so does everyone else in the castle, not only the child, but her entire world goes off to sleep; quoting the Brothers Grimm: *"And this sleep fell upon the whole castle; the king and queen who had returned and were in the great hall, fell fast asleep, and with them the whole court. The horses in the stalls, the dogs in the yard, the pigeons on the roof, the flies on the wall, the very fire that flickers on the hearth, became still, and slept like the rest; and the meat on the spit ceased roasting, and the cook, who was going to pull the scullion's hair for some mistake he had made, let him go, and went to sleep. And the wind ceased, not a leaf fell from the trees about the castle."*[1]

The second reason, of much greater significance to me, is that the sleeping princess is awakened by a kiss from the prince. Who or what is this prince and what meaning could be placed in the simple act of a kiss especially in regards to organizations?

As I grew from a young boy of fairy tales into a man, world-weary from life's realities, I thought the story of sleeping beauty had much more meaning beneath the surface. I began to search for the significance of sleep spoken of in the story. Was this fairy tale simply a children's story of kings, queens, princes and princesses who roamed the land or could I apply it to the psychological and spiritual

---

1 The Brothers Grim (1812) *The Sleeping Beauty.* Little Briar Rose.

world of my work; connections between CEO's, senior management, strategic plans and employees? It was at this time that I began to sense something about my attitude towards my work life; a stirring that would flow into my consciousness at the oddest times, affecting all my relationships. And this concept of sleep began to take on an organizational perspective of the dysfunction I was experiencing in my workplace as I began to ask, what puts the princess (me) and everyone else in the kingdom (the organizations I worked in) to sleep and was the sleep in this fairy tale speaking to just that dysfunction?

"The woods are lovely, dark, and deep, But I have promises to keep, And miles to go before I sleep, And miles to go before I sleep."

Robert Frost

Chapter 4

How do I know I am asleep?

While driving home one day listening to a motivating lecture on CD, I realized that I had just missed an important piece of the speaker's message. I "rewound" the CD and a short time later once again realized I had missed the exact same section. With much determination, I "rewound" it once again with the conviction of hearing all of it, this time "come hell or high water." Well, after many miles down the road I pulled into my driveway "waking up" only to notice that I was in "high water" and the part that I wanted to hear had long since passed. Where had I gone, not just once but three times, and what phenomenon would take me away within seconds from something I deemed so important? You may ask what this has to do with organizations. My simple answer is; everything. How we "travel" through our work and our ability to remember what is important, reveals our habits in the organization. If we accept this, the question then becomes how do we awaken and get the tools needed for our journey?

In this day and age, we seem to have all the information we need to improve our organizations; books and CD's on organizational development, culture change committees, orientations, stimulating workshops and motivational speakers, which all address what makes an organization great. With all this information, what could possibly be the real difficulty we face? Is it possible that all our self-help books, our workshops and motivational speakers are merely band-aids on a deep wound and may even contribute to the depth of our sleep? So, what is one to do and is there a parallel between our fairy tale and real life? With this question, we are touching upon something central: just as the princess falls asleep, so do we. And if I am asleep is the whole world sleeping with me, including the organization I work in?

What an odd and inconceivable thought it is that we might be sound asleep. Everything suggests otherwise. My eyes are open; I have awareness of my movements, my thoughts, my feelings. But if I look back at the countless moments that make up my day, I begin to realize how few of them I remember. I may remember the argument with a fellow employee, the crushing deadline, the stubbed toe or the beautiful sunrise, but there are so many more events that have gone by.

It is as if we are literally sleep-walking through life and work.

"The only person you are destined to become is the person you decide to be"

Ralph Waldo Emerson

Chapter 5

From Whence It Came

Before exploring the influences this theory has on organizations, it would be good to understand where this belief comes from. There are numerous references to the idea of sleep in many wisdom traditions, but the one that is most connected to our particular journey originates in ancient Greece.

In Greek mythology, there is reference to a river with the unlikely name of Lethe. The word means "forgetfulness" and is the root for our word lethargy. It is also related to the Greek word for truth, Alethia or un-forgetfulness. The river of Lethe, in Greek mythology, flows through a cave which goes by the name of The Cave of Sleep and it is told that if one drank from this river that one would experience complete forgetfulness. In Greek tradition, there is a correlation between forgetfulness, sleep, and truth and from this perspective, if we want to get to the truth, we will have to remember something: but what is it that we need to remember? In a strange and unlikely way, as we begin to explore these caves of sleep and rivers of forgetfulness, our vision of an organization's search for excellence expands according to our ability to understand not so much what we do, but what we forget to do.

My simple premise is that organizations are not only drinking from this river of forgetfulness, but are so immersed in it that they are as oblivious to this phenomenon as we are to the air we breathe. The ability to remember the things that are deemed most important is crucial to an organization's health and well-being: forgetfulness pulls it further and further down the river and where this river leads is to a mythical tale called Sleeping Beauty. The ability to remember that we are asleep becomes a fundamental imperative and instead of now passively flowing with its current; we are given the chance to be kissed by the prince.

That we do not remember should be obvious but in fact it is not. In Sleeping Beauty, the princess and her kingdom slept for 100 years, virtually a lifetime. The implication is that maybe we too sleep our life away. In the funny and inspiring movie, City Slickers, Billy Crystal's character, Mitch, while riding herd with a crusty old cowboy, speaks to the question of forgetfulness this way:

Cowboy: Do you want me to tell you the secret of life?

Mitch: What is it?

Cowboy: (Holding up his index finger) it's this.

Mitch: It's a finger?

Cowboy: No, it's one thing, just one thing. You stick to that and everything else don't mean shit.

Mitch: That's great but what is the one thing?

Cowboy: That's what you have to figure out.

From an organizational standpoint, the cowboy is onto something essential, and most companies seem to feel that they have this figured out and support this feeling by circulating a document which they call a mission statement. Welcome to the world of sleep.

"Through memory we travel against time,
Through forgetfulness we follow its course."

Joseph Joubert (1754-1824)

Chapter 6

Straying from the Mission

After observing O Sensei, the founder of Aikido, sparring with an accomplished fighter, a young student said to the master,

"You never lose your balance, what is your secret?"

"You are wrong," O Sensei replied, *"I am constantly losing my balance. My skill lies in my ability to regain it."* [2]

Whether it is a Sensei or CEO, department manager or front-line employee, what a different world we would live in if we could cultivate the skill of regaining our balance. What our young student observes is a shallow impression of what is actually happening; underneath lays the world we are trying to enter. The ancient Greek philosophers saw this in the personality and deemed this personality as illusionary, merely a mask of who we really are. They understood that what we see in a person from the outside is very different than what is going on inside. When we see another person or a co-worker, we are most often looking at this mask. So, as we observe CEO's, senior management and colleagues, it may seem like they have it all together, but inwardly, where it counts the most, they are losing their balance and forgetting what it is that is important in the organization. A new employee could now be saying to senior management:

"O Senior Management; you never forget the organization's mission, vision, and values. What is you secret?"

And in an organization of excellence, Senior Management would respond:

---

2   Stone, Paton, Heed, (2000) **Difficult Conversations,** New York, Penguin Books

17

"You are wrong. I am constantly losing them; my skill lies in my ability to regain them."

Cowboys or sensei, CEO's or front-line employees, what an extraordinary world we would live in if we could remember this reality.

When the cowboy says "it's one thing," he is acknowledging a universal truth and in organizations we all know this 'one thing' as the mission statement. The mission statement's responsibility is to determine the milieu of everything the organization does and addresses the question of what it is trying to accomplish. This is where most organizations start and it is not a bad place to begin; unfortunately, it is also the place where most organizations stop. Having a mission statement is enough for them. Again, we are welcomed to the world of sleep.

Our sleep becomes even deeper because the truth is that we are more apt to follow our own mission, spurred on by our own vision which incorporates our own values more than the organization's ideals. Social scientist, Harrington Emerson said it this way, "Workers at the lower end of line organizations (feel) so far from those who dictate policies…that they are driven to create minor ideals and inspirations of their own, these often in variance with the ideals of those above them." So, whether we view sleep from the eyes of Sleeping Beauty, O Sensei, or a social scientist, we are exploring the theme of forgetfulness in our own particular way. We hear all of them speaking to either what is happening, why it happens, or how it happens. The what, why, and how, varies from organization to organization; that it happens is undeniable.

"We Sow A Thought and Reap an Act;
We Sow an Act and Reap A Habit;
We Sow A Habit and Reap A Character;
We Sow a Character and Reap a Destiny."

Ralph Waldo Emerson

Chapter 7

The Cave of Sleep

What is it that not only brings us to the banks of the river Lethe but also casts us into its current, sending us on our way downstream into forgetfulness? What is it that makes us sleep and in sleeping makes us forget? One answer comes from a source that is over 2300 years old. That source is Aristotle. I can hear the moans all over the business world as the name is uttered but who better to study a Greek river called Lethe.

In ancient Greece, an extraordinary phenomenon was underway. People were engaged in the study of why people do the things they do. Moreover, a number of these individuals, Aristotle being one of them, came to this interesting conclusion as condensed by Will Durant in his book "The Story Of Philosophy"

> **"We are what we repeatedly do;
> excellence then is not an act, but a habit."[3]**

There it is in the proverbial nut shell, both simple and elegant. I remember the first time I read this quote, where I was in the work-place and how strongly it affected me. It has become the impetus for a life long journey and central to my understanding of organizational excellence. What makes an organization excellent is not only our ability to read the writing on the wall (mission statement) but to live it. Many mission statements use the word excellence or a synonym of it to signify their highest desire or goal. Aristotle simply says that

---

3 Durant, Will (1967), *The Story of Philosophy,* Simon & Schuster; Revised edition

whatever word you use, what makes it true is the ability to repeat it, to make it a habit, or in O Sensei language, the ability to regain it. This understanding forms the guiding principles and behaviors that dictate how the organization and its people are expected to operate.

Aristotle continues, *"... in our transactions with other men"* (co-workers) *"it is by action that some become just and others unjust, and it is by acting in the face of danger and by developing the habit of feeling fear or confidence that some become brave men or cowards"* (good workers or not). *"The same applies to the appetites and feelings of anger, by reacting in one way or another to given circumstances, some people become self-controlled and gentle, and others self-indulgent and short-tempered"* (something we see in organizations all the time). *"In a word, characteristics develop from corresponding activities."* [4]

Furthermore, *"for that reason we must see to it that our activities are of a certain kind, since any variations are reflected in our characteristics. Hence"* (and this is the crux of Aristotle's message) *"it is no small matter whether one habit or another is inculcated in us from early childhood; on the contrary, it makes a considerable difference, or, rather, all the difference."* [5]

As we look around and begin to notice the environment we work in, what Aristotle is saying becomes the basis from which the rest of our story unfolds and it will make all the difference how it ends.

---

4   Ostwald, Martin. (1962) *Aristotle Nicomachean Ethics,* Indianapolis, Bobbs-Merrill Educational Publishing, 1103b 14-22.
5   Ibid, 1103b 22-25

"People need to be reminded more often than they
need to be instructed"

Samuel Johnson

Chapter 8

More than a Game

Allow me to move forward 2300 years and bring home Aristotle's point using America's favorite pastime, the game of baseball, and let's connect Aristotle, Sleeping Beauty and baseball to the work we do.

Many baseball players develop certain habits or rituals during the season to avoid bad luck or just to make them feel more comfortable. I remember doing this as a young boy. I had to take just so many practice swings before the pitch (three to be exact) or needed to adjust my helmet in a certain way, much like big league players do today. It did not necessarily make me play better but it did make me feel as if I was more in charge of the situation. People in organizations tend to do the same things with their behaviors and attitudes. It may not be helpful to behave in such a way or speak with a certain attitude but it is for them a "comfortable" way to interact and dare I say, play the game. They are in many ways adjusting their helmets and these adjustments create their contentment but not necessarily the contentment of others. We can go back more than 2300 years and realize that not much has changed. To continue with Aristotle *"for the things which we have to learn before we can do them, we learn by doing: men become builders by building houses and harpists by playing the harp. Similarly, we become just by the practice of just actions, self-controlled by exercising self-control, and courageous by performing acts of courage."* [6]

6   Ostwald, M. (1962) *Aristotle Nicomachean Ethics*, Indianapolis, Bobbs-Merrill Educational Publishing, 1103a32-1103b1

In other words, strangely, we do what we do because we already do it. Attitude begets attitude, behavior begets behavior and habit begets habit. Notice the habits of the workplace where you work and then notice when change is asked for. Even with orientations, workshops, and all the in-services, human nature has the tendency to want to continue on the same path, the one already there. The approach we take to fulfill our organization's mission, vision, and values are just "those habits of a certain kind" and "reflects our characteristics" and it is through the behaviors of front-line employees, middle management, and senior team members that we come to know what the mission is. Our behaviors, like a default switch in the brain (or in fairy tale language our capacity to fall asleep as if under a spell) are simply a habit of either the mind, emotions or body that reflects these characteristics. If we accept this reality, we are less inclined to take the actions of our co-workers personally. We may not like what they do but we see that they have learned these behaviors by repeatedly doing them. This may be why so many well-intentioned books suggesting better ways for organizations to perform, eventually find their way to a bookshelf graveyard while we go back to what we do so easily,

as if we could do it in our sleep,
because we do.

Each kingdom has its own way of going to sleep, in our story the kingdom began its slumber thus; *"The Queen gave birth to a little girl who was so very beautiful that the King could not contain himself for joy, and so he prepared a great feast. He invited all his friends, relatives, and noble acquaintances, and also the fairy women, so that they might be kindly disposed towards the child. Unfortunately, there were thirteen of these fairies in the kingdom, and the King owned only twelve golden plates. He was ashamed and afraid to ask one of them to dine from a silver plate. Therefore, the oldest and most difficult of the fairies was not invited, and the King was secretly glad of an excuse to exclude her from the company." [7]*

So, the King is ashamed and afraid. A King no less. This has the distinct echo of the story of O Sensei. It is an illusion to think that O Sensei is not expected to be off balance or to think that Kings are not expected to be ashamed and afraid, but this is exactly what we bring to our organizations. The King's way of thinking is his habit of eating off the finest plate and rationalizing his attitude toward this one fairy. Think of all the trouble he would have avoided to the kingdom and his daughter, if he had chosen the silver plate for himself. It is the same for CEO's, middle management, or front-line workers and the longer we stay in this illusion, the more dysfunctional we become. Our inability to fulfill our dinner plans (habits) often lead to unintended consequences.

When the King learns that his daughter would fall into a long sleep after pricking her finger on a spindle, he responds in this way: *"The poor King became distraught with grief and dispair and in an attempt to avert the unhappy fate pronounced by the old fairy, at once published an edict forbidding all persons to use a spinning wheel or keep a spindle in the house. [8]*

The King does what he does, not because it is the wise or sensible thing to do, but because he has the power to do it. In Aristotelian terms this becomes the difference between what is called an apparent good (something that looks good in the moment) and a genuine good. We all know people within our organizations who subscribe to

---

7   Hyman, T.S. (1977) *The Sleeping Beauty,* Boston, Toronto, Little, Brown and Company.
8   Perrault, Charles, (1697) *The Sleeping Beauty in the Woods.*

the apparent good and better still we have all experienced it ourselves at one time or another. We tend to look at this exclusively as senior leadership's dilemma and fail to understand that within the organization, at different times and with different people, everyone exhibits this apparent good. This then becomes the organization's shadow. Each individual begins to builds their own inner kingdom (Emerson's minor ideals) and create a world of alternatives which often conflict with those of the organization.

How do we come to such a place? What has changed for the King that begets such a reactive response and belief? In another version of Sleeping Beauty this belief is set in motion this way: *"everything that the heart could wish for was theirs. They were rich, they lived in a wonderful palace full of the costliest treasures, their kingdom was at peace, and their people were prosperous."* [9] This, in a psychological way, is the way we are born into everything, be it life, relationship, or the job we desire. There is a sense of prosperity and peace at the newness of things and if we stay open to this experience, it becomes the genuine good we seek, but if we come to it from relieving fear and anxiety, as the King did, it becomes an apparent good and lasts for only a short time (sometimes with dire consequences as we will see). Looking at an organization as a kingdom, all the inner characteristics (habits) that accumulate begin to form into behaviors that dictate the direction of our work life, and as with the King, organizations contain similar traits. The fear of loss and conflict speaks to our inability to have the difficult conversations we need to have. What else would possess a man of power to destroy such an integral way of life?

So, this is where we find the king *"after seven years had passed the King gradually forgot about the dreadful curse, and was finally*

9   Evans,C.S. *The Sleeping Beauty*, Viking Press 1972

content." [10] In our own way, whether CEO, senior leaders, or front-line employees, we all think we are Kings. We invalidate and devalue the kingdom around us, making those circumstances fit into our comfortable realm and forgetting our mission. Being self-righteous we feel content and, in this contentment, we forget. We know what happened to the princess even with all the King's precautions.

10   Hyman, T.S. (1977) *The Sleeping Beauty*, Boston, Toronto, Little, Brown and Company.

"The breeze at dawn has secrets to tell you
Don't go back to sleep.
You must ask for what you really want
Don't go back to sleep.
People are going back and forth across the doorsill
where the two worlds touch,
The door is round and open
Don't go back to sleep."

Rumi

Chapter 9

Purpose

If you have come this far, from an organizational standpoint, you are one odd duck. Odd you are because not many in today's workplace are as curious as you about the [ever present] absurdities that take place at work. It is a curiosity much like what we have when we read a fairy tale and just like in a fairy tale, we wait for that twist in the story that shows us a different direction.

Going back 2300 years, there was an intense debate going on in Greece. It is a debate which goes right to the heart of organizational dysfunction and revolves around how excellence (there's that word again) is acquired. On one side of this "argument" is the intellectual understanding of Socrates who felt that if someone truly knew something was good and right, that person would by necessity of virtue be compelled to do it. As Aristotle describes it, *"Socrates, for example, believed that it would be strange if, when a man possesses knowledge, something else should overpower it and drag it about like a slave. In fact, Socrates was completely opposed to the view (that a man may know what is right but do what is wrong), and did not believe that moral weakness exists. He claimed that no one acts contrary to what is best in the conviction (that what he is doing is bad), but through ignorance (of the fact that it is bad.)"* [11]

Our modern culture has perverted this view of Socrates' into what is called "the mission statement on the wall syndrome." It assumes that just because we have read it, we will do it. In many

---

11   Ostwald, Martin. (1962) **Aristotle Nicomachean Ethics,** Indianapolis, Bobbs-Merrill Educational Publishing, 1145b 22-27.

modern organizations, this view even goes so far as to assume that since we have state of the art workshops, the best motivational speakers, and volumes of books that explain everything from soup to nuts about building a better organization, going from "good to great" is inevitable.

On the other side of this debate, Aristotle thought it was all well and good to know, but knowing wasn't enough. For Aristotle, it was in the doing that one brought this ability to completion and fulfillment, and into habit. *"Now this theory is plainly at variance with the observed facts, and one ought to investigate the emotion (involved in the acts of a morally weak man): if it comes through ignorance, what manner of ignorance is it? For evidently a man who is morally weak in his actions does not think (that he ought to act the way he does) before he is in the grip of emotion."* [12] Most organizations, unfortunately, subscribe to Socrates' theory.

Another subtle theme that runs throughout the tale is that many a prince had tried over the years to rescue the princess and failed. *"And so, after many years, the legend spread abroad to neighboring countries, and many a young prince dreamed that it was he who was destined to break the spell and waken the sleeping princess. Now and again one would take the quest upon him and try to force his way through the thick hedge. But no one succeeded. The sharp thorns gripped the unhappy young men like clutching hands, and held them fast, so that they could neither go forward nor back, and they perished miserably. Their bones, whitened by the sun and wind, remained there as a warning for all to see, and the creeping plants grew over them."* [13]

---

12 Ostwald, Martin. (1962) *Aristotle Nicomachean Ethics,* Indianapolis, Bobbs-Merrill Educational Publishing, 1145b 28-30.

13 Evans, C.S. (1920) The Sleeping Beauty, London, William Heinemann, Philadelphia, J.B. Lippincott.

So, it is with our feeble understanding of cultural change or our ability to rescue sleeping beauty. We are at best ill prepared to take on this quest and being ill prepared we have the tendency to "force our way through" and do more harm than good. Finding ourselves amongst the "sharp thorns" is not in and of itself bad. These "sharp thorns" can, in one sense, be what "holds us fast," and in another sense, they can be our wakeup call, that leads up to what we know as the kiss from the prince. In this same sense, these sharp thorns hold fast an organization in its quest for excellence and whether it grows or perishes.

We reach a critical point in our story, for this is the moment where the organization and individual meet on somewhat equal terms, a rather unusual place for both, and it is at this precise point we ask what could possibly be the purpose of this story. *"The purpose of the present study is not, as it is in other inquires, the attainment of theoretical knowledge: we are not conducting this inquiry in order to know what virtue is, but in order to become good, else there would be no advantage in studying it. For that reason, it becomes necessary to examine the problem of actions, and to ask how they are to be performed. For, as we have said, the actions determine what kinds of characteristics are developed."*[14]

In our fairy tale, many have tried and failed to rescue the princess and we should be curious as to what it is that will make this particular prince succeed where all others have failed. In every fairy tale, the main character is called to action and this action is fraught with dilemmas and choice. It is here we come to the central theme of Aristotle's Ethics as well as the origin of the mission statement. *"If in all our conduct, then, there is some end that we wish on its own account, choosing everything as a means to it; then clearly this one*

---

14 Ostwald, Martin. (1962) *Aristotle Nicomachean Ethics*, Indianapolis, Bobbs-Merrill Educational Publishing, 1103b 25-30.

end must be the good, even indeed, the highest good. Will not knowl-edge of it, then, have an important influence on our lives? Will it not better enable us to hit the right mark, like archers who have a defi-nite target to aim at? If so, we must try to comprehend, in outline at least, what that highest end is." [15] So, over the centuries the cowboy and Aristotle meet and help us to define what a mission statement is.

Cowboy: Do you want me to tell you what the secret of life is?

Mitch: What is it?

Cowboy: It's one thing. Just one thing. You stick to that and everything else don't mean shit.

15 Wheelwright (1935) Aristotle, Indianapolis, Bobbs-Merrill Educational Publishing.

Alice came to a fork in the road.
"Which road do I take?" She asked.
"Where do you want to go?" responded the Cheshire cat.
"I don't know," Alice answered
"Then," said the cat, "it doesn't matter."

Lewis Carroll

Chapter 10

Choice

In the Harvard Business Review's 10 Must Reads on Leadership, one of the articles speaks of the scale of our sleep this way; *"Executives have a good reason to be scared. You can't do anything in business without followers. So, executives had better know what it takes to lead effectively-they must find ways to engage people and rouse their commitment to company goals. But most don't know how, and who can blame them? There's simply too much advice out there. Last year alone, more than 2000 books on leadership were published."* [16] Two thousand books on leadership in one year! With so much information out there, how can we say we are not missing something fundamental in our approach to organizational culture? It is only with a considerable amount of awareness that we come to see we are much more ready to be instructed than to be reminded and that this instruction has a fundamental flaw within it. This is the place where our Sleeping Beauty waits for the kiss.

All through our story there is a constant reference to habits and Aristotle's claim that through these habits is the path to excellence. How can this be so? In this day and age, we think of habits as negative, something to avoid and more importantly as the lack of choice. How is it that changing one habit for another could create choice and from an organizational perspective, excellence. It is here that our fairy tale and Aristotle's philosophy become aligned. As in all good fairy tales something logical is always turned on its head and what seems absurd in one instance now becomes sensible. Aristotle is doing the same by suggesting that habit does not decrease choice as

16   Goffee, R., and G. Jones, (2000) Harvard Business Review, *Why Should Anyone Be Led By you*, Pg 79.

one would think, but turned on its head, increases choice. Finally, we come to what, in our fairy tale, becomes the KISS, the moment of waking up from our sleep. Where has it been all along and what is this habit of a special kind? In order to answer, we need to begin again.

Once upon a time in a land far away lived an organization. In this organization were many good people of different shapes, sizes, and dispositions, who wanted only the best for themselves and the people they loved. However, even with their best intentions, something strange seemed to happen to all of these good people, as if under a spell, they fell sound asleep. Now it certainly did not look as if they were asleep. They continued to move, have conversations, and even get a paycheck at the end of the week, but alas, asleep they were. Their sleep was not a sleep in the usual sense of lying in bed with eyes closed but the kind of sleep one recognizes upon waking from a daydream. And during this daydream, all these good people, did their work, had their meetings and took their breaks as if the dream they were in was real. One day, some of these good people, as if arising from their nightly sleep, began to open their eyes and asked themselves, am I dreaming. And as this question persisted, some of these good people, in a restless state, trying to awaken from that dream, began to get an uneasy feeling, a most uncomfortable feeling, and a sense that this is not the way it is supposed to be. Along with this uneasiness, something began to stir, and certain individuals, faintly at first began to hear an echo; an echo coming from somewhere deep within each one of them. This echo started as a simple vibration and began to get louder, forming words, and as the words became clearer their eyes opened with understanding, and they began to smile inside as they realized what was being said;

choose your habit, do not let it choose you.

We use habit to escape from habit and paraphrasing Arthur Young, "In the midst of this thistle of habit, we pluck the flower of freedom."

Our ability to hear this call is a prerequisite for all that comes later and it is only here that one can truly make those decisions that will allow us to "live happily ever after." Once again and maybe for the final time in our story we hear Aristotle, **"It must be observed that the nature of moral qualities is such that they are destroyed by defect and by excess. We see the same thing happen in the case of strength and of health, to illustrate, as we must, the invisible by means of the visible examples: excess as well as deficiency of physical exercise destroys our strength, and similarly, too much and too little food and drink destroys our health; the proportionate amount, however, produces, increases and preserves it."[17]** We may thus conclude that … **"excellence is a characteristic involving choice, and it consists in observing the mean relative to us, a mean which is defined by a rational principle, such as a man of practical wisdom would use to determine it."[18]**

So our story, as we journey to find the princess, no longer becomes what needs to be done, (because this has been captured time and again in countless books) or even how to go about doing it but more

17 Ostwald, Martin. (1962) *Aristotle Nicomachean Ethics*, Indianapolis, Bobbs-Merrill Educational Publishing, 1104a11-19.

18 Ibid 1106b36-1107a2.

importantly, as we bow and pucker our lips for the fulfillment of that one powerful moment, we do one of the most eloquent acts in creation,

we notice that we are doing it.

It is with this act that we become conscious of our own particular fairy tale, which we called life. We start to realize that it is life that leads us into habit and it is also life that brings us out. For Aristotle, the choice that brought us out of habit became known as the golden mean, that place between the extremes of excess and deficiency. What brings us to this golden mean is the same thing that draws us away from it, our life, in organizational language it is our work. In the fairy tale it sounds like this:

"I am seeking the Sleeping Beauty."

"Do you love her more than life itself?" asked the dwarf.

"I am prepared to forfeit my life to find her," said the prince.

Forfeit my life? Is it only in a fairy tale that we could imagine hearing such a concept? In an organization we would be saying, I am willing to forfeit my habit for something better. We have our duties to do and lists to maintain, orientations and workshops to attend, as well as hundreds of other necessary (and not so necessary) things to make us feel we are competent to compete in this modern world, but somehow in the end we still have this nagging feeling we are sleeping. The question now becomes how do we change this habit for the organization's mission and still maintain our balance? It is not the automatic habits of a sleepwalking person that we are looking for but the habit of choosing the mean between too much and too little of anything.

I end as I began, a young man traveling down the road listening to a CD and sensing that I have forgotten something, but this time with the help of our fairy tale something different begins to happen. *"At last he came into a chamber all gilded with gold, where he saw upon a bed, the curtains of which were all open, the finest sight was ever beheld: a princess, whose bright, and in a manner resplendent beauty, had somewhat in it divine. He approached with trembling and admiration and falling down before her upon his knees gave her a kiss."* [19] As soon as he touched her, the spell was broken.

The spell is broken, the princess awakes and the kingdom soon comes back to life. The spell is broken because we begin to notice that it is not just anyone who is getting the kiss, it is me who is getting it. But this is something we already knew; we just needed a fairy tale to remind us.

"After a little while, they went down from the tower together, hand and hand. Where one drop of blood drains a castle of life, so one kiss can bring it alive again. Then the King and Queen woke up, so did all their knights and ladies, everyone looked at each other with astonishment in their sleepy eyes. The horses in the stables stood up and shook themselves, and the grooms scratched their heads and stretched their legs. The hounds began to leap about, barking at nothing and wagging their tails. The rooster called a belated and mighty crow to his hens, and the doves on the roof lifted their heads from under their wings, looked surprise, and flew off into the fields. The flies on the wall began to crawl and the fire crackled up to roast

---

19   Perrault, Charles, (1697) *The Sleeping Beauty in the Woods.*

41

the meat. The cook blinked his eyes and then boxed the scullion's ears so soundly that the poor boy cursed and howled. The kitchen maid went back to plucking the fowl, and even the very stones of the palace slowly began to breathe again." [20]

We are now alive but not in the old sense. Something real has taken hold and we see a new way of living and working and we begin to breathe again and the excellence we have talked so often about now becomes a habit worth waking up too.

**"...The princess awoke and bestowed upon him a look
more tender than a first glance might seem to warrant.**

**'Is it you, dear prince?' she said. 'You have been
long in coming!'"** [21]

20   Hyman, T.S. (1977) *The Sleeping Beauty*, Boston, Toronto, Little, Brown and Company.

21   Perrault, Charles, (1697) *The Sleeping Beauty in the Woods.*

Bibliography

The Brothers Grim (1812) *The Sleeping Beauty*. Little Briar Rose.

Durant, Will (1967), **The Story of Philosophy,** Simon & Schuster; Revised edition.

Evans, C.S. (1920) *The Sleeping Beauty*, London, William Heinemann, Philadelphia, J.B. Lippincott.

Goffee, R., Jones, G. (2000) Harvard Business Review, **Why Should Anyone Be Led By you**, Pg 79.

Hyman, T.S. (1977) *The Sleeping Beauty*, Boston, Toronto, Little, Brown and Company.

Ostwald, Martin (1962) **Aristotle Nicomachean Ethics**, Indianapolis, Bobbs-Merrill Educational Publishing.

Meyer, Mercer (1984) **Sleeping Beauty,** New York MacMillan Publishing Company.

Perrault, Charles (1697) *The Sleeping Beauty in the Woods*.

Stone, Paton, Heed (2000) **Difficult Conversations**, New York, Penguin Books.

Wheelwright (1935) **Aristotle**, Indianapolis, Bobbs-Merrill Educational Publishing.

Stephen Capizzano

I am a DREAMER. I have always been a dreamer and at my age probably will always be one. My dreaming has been interrupted by an MS in Healthcare Administration, a Healthcare career and as a team member for the Malcolm Baldrige Performance Excellence Program; a program that recognizes performance excellence in organizations. I have also facilitated many groups in their journey to practical human transformation.

Born into a working-class family, I remember a summer when I was going to quit school. My father got me a job where he worked helping to build submarines. He arranged it so that all summer I stood on top of a submarine, under the hot summer sun, in full protective gear, sand blasting. After that summer, I went back to school. I continually thank my father for the lesson and guidepost he so gently put in front of me.

Even with all this dreaming and life experience, I still search, with immense gratitude, for a deeper meaning of life. This fairytale is about this search.

For question or inquiries please contact the author at:
forgetfulorganization@gmail.com